NO FRILLS Exam Prep Books

Intellectual Properties, Trademarks and Copyrights

Contents Update

All books come with LIFE TIME FREE UPDATES. When you find a newer version of the purchased book all you need to do is to go and download. **Please check our web site's Free Updates section regularly:**

http://www.examreview.net/free_updates.htm

Page Formatting and Typeface

To accommodate the needs of those with weaker vision, we use LARGER PRINT throughout the book whenever practical. The text in this book was created using Garamond (size 16). A little bit of page resizing, however, may have happened along the actual book printing process.

The Exam

The Certified Quality Auditor exam candidate is expected to know the standards and principles of auditing as well as the auditing techniques of examining, questioning, evaluating and reporting to determine the adequacy and deficiencies of a quality system.

We create these self-practice test questions referencing the concepts and principles currently valid in the exam. Each question comes with an answer and a short explanation which aids you in seeking further study information. For purpose of exam readiness drilling, this product includes questions that have varying numbers of choices. Some have 2 while some have 5 or 6. We want to make sure these questions are tough enough to really test your readiness and draw your focus to the weak areas. Think of these as challenges presented to you so to assess your comprehension of the subject matters. The goal is to reinforce learning, to validate successful transference of knowledge and to identify areas of weakness that require remediation. The questions are NOT designed to "simulate" actual exam questions. "realistic" or actual questions that are for cheating purpose are not available in any of our products.

Question 1

"Quality":

Possible choices:

is a subjective term.

is an objective term.

ANSWER:

According to ASQ, "Quality" is a subjective term for which each person has his or her own definition.

Question 2

The Continuous Quality Improvement paradigm was first effectively demonstrated in:

Possible choices:

USA

UK

Japan

Korea

China

None of the choices.

ANSWER:

The Continuous Quality Improvement paradigm was promoted by quality experts like Deming and Juran, and was first effectively demonstrated in the industries of post-war Japan.

Question 3

Which of the following is a data-driven systematic approach to solving problem with a focus on customer impact?

Possible choices:

APQP

DFSS

Six Sigma

GMP

Fishbone

Kaizen

PDCA

None of the choices.

ANSWER:

Originally developed by Motorola, Six Sigma is a business improvement methodology. The core of this methodology is a data-driven systematic approach to solving problem (with a focus on customer impact).

Question 4

With Six Sigma, which role is responsible for integrating Six Sigma implementation across the organization?

Possible choices:

Champions

Master Black Belts

Black Belts

Green Belts

Red Belts

None of the choices.

ANSWER:

Six Sigma identifies several key roles. Champions are responsible for integrating Six Sigma implementation across the organization. Master Black Belts act as in-house expert coach for the organization on Six Sigma. Black Belts operate under Master Black Belts to apply Six Sigma methodology to specific projects. Green Belts take up Six Sigma implementation along with their other job responsibilities.

Question 5

Quality Assurance is supposed to cover what activities (choose all that apply):

Possible choices:

design

development

production

installation

servicing

documentation

None of the choices.

ANSWER:

Quality Assurance is supposed to cover all activities from design, development, production, installation, servicing and documentation. It includes the regulation of the quality of raw materials, assemblies, products and components; services related to production; and management, production, and inspection processes.

Question 6

Which of the following is a document that details the corporate quality policy and the corresponding structure of the organization?

Possible choices:

Quality Manual

Quality Charter

Quality Policy

Quality Statement

None of the choices.

ANSWER:

A Quality Manual is a document that details the corporate quality policy and the corresponding structure of the organization. A good quality manual should reference all of the appropriate Operating Procedures.

Question 7

The _____ is a graphical depiction of loss.

Possible choices:

Taguchi Loss

Ishikawa

Kaizen

Kaizen Blitz

Muda

Scrum

Poka-yoke

None of the choices.

ANSWER:

The Taguchi Loss Function is a graphical depiction of loss. Developed by the Japanese business statistician Genichi Taguchi, it describes a phenomenon affecting the value of products produced by a company.

Question 8

Which of the following refers to the framework of procedures and techniques for developing products in industry such as the automotive industry?

Possible choices:

APQP

DFSS

Six Sigma

GMP

Fishbone

Kaizen

PDCA

None of the choices.

ANSWER:

Advanced Product Quality Planning (APQP) refers to the framework of procedures and techniques for developing products in industry such as the automotive industry. It is in a sense quite similar to the concept of Design For Six Sigma (DFSS).

Question 9

The sample size required really depends on (choose all that apply):

Possible choices:

the nature of the analysis

the desired precision of the estimates

the kind of statistical comparisons to be made

the number of variables to be examined

the heterogeneity of the sampled universe

None of the choices.

ANSWER:

Talking about sampling, it is believed that the sample size required really depends on the nature of the analysis, the desired precision of the estimates, the kind of statistical comparisons to be made, the number of variables to be examined and the heterogeneity of the sampled universe.

Question 10

Which of the following is well recognized worldwide for quality control testing of foods and pharmaceutical products?

Possible choices:

APQP

DFSS

Six Sigma

GMP

Fishbone

Kaizen

PDCA

None of the choices.

ANSWER:

The Good Manufacturing Practice (GMP) is recognized worldwide for quality control testing of foods and pharmaceutical products. It takes a holistic approach of regulating the manufacturing and laboratory testing environment itself. It emphasizes the documentation of every aspect of the process involved with drug and medical device manufacture.

Question 11

An Ishikawa diagram is also called a _____ diagram.

Possible choices:

APQP

DFSS

Six Sigma

GMP

Fishbone

Kaizen

PDCA

None of the choices.

ANSWER:

An Ishikawa diagram looks like a fishbone so that's why it is also called a fishbone diagram. You want to use it to reveal key relationship among various variables and possible causes provide additional insight into process behavior.

Question 12

In a typical fishbone diagram, 6 Ms include (choose all that apply):

Possible choices:

Machine ✓

Method ✓

Materials ✓

Measurement ✓

Man ✓

Mother Nature ✓

None of the choices.

ANSWER:

Causes in a typical fishbone diagram are arranged into main categories such as the 6 M (Machine, Method, Materials, Measurement, Man and Mother Nature), the 8 P (Price, Promotion, People, Processes, Place / Plant, Policies, Procedures & Products), and the 4 S (Surroundings, Suppliers, Systems, Skills). You don't use it when the team size is too small for brainstorming or when the problem is too simple (Fishbone is used primarily for handling complicated problems anyway).

Question 13

Which of the following is a Japanese word for "change for the better"?

Possible choices:

Taguchi Loss

Ishikawa

Kaizen

Kaizen Blitz

Muda

Scrum

Poka-yoke

None of the choices.

ANSWER:

Kaizen is a Japanese word for "change for the better". It refers to an approach to productivity improvement originating in applications of the work of American experts like Frederick Taylor and Edwards Deming. The major goals of kaizen include and not limit to elimination of waste, just-in-time delivery, standardized work and paced moving lines.

Question 14

The cycle of kaizen activity includes several "stages". Which of the following is the first stage?

Possible choices:

standardize an operation

measure the standardized operation

gauge measurements against requirements

innovate to meet requirements and increase productivity

standardize the new, improved operations

continue cycle

None of the choices.

ANSWER:

The cycle of kaizen activity includes several "stages": standardize an operation -> measure the standardized operation -> gauge measurements against requirements -> innovate to meet requirements and increase productivity -> standardize the new, improved operations -> continue cycle. People often refer to this cycle as the Shewhart cycle, Deming cycle, or PDCA.

Question 15

The foundation elements of Kaizen include (choose all that apply):

Possible choices:

Team work

Personal Discipline

Improved morale

Quality circles

Suggestions for improvement

None of the choices.

ANSWER:

The foundation elements of Kaizen include: Team work, Personal Discipline, Improved morale, Quality circles, and Suggestions for improvement.

Question 16

Kaizen is a daily activity.

Possible choices:

True

False

ANSWER:

True. Kaizen is a daily activity - when done correctly it can humanize the workplace. This is due to the fact that kaizen emphasizes three principles: process and results together, not results alone; systemic thinking on the big picture; and a non-blaming culture.

Question 17

The Kaizen Blitz:

Possible choices:

is short-term

is mid-term

is long-term

ANSWER:

The Kaizen Blitz (aka Kaizen Event) is a focused, short-term (2-10 days) project for improving a process. It typically includes training followed by analysis, design, and, often, re-arrangement of a product line or area. Process and Value Stream Mapping are heavily being relied upon on for it.

Question 18

_____ Events refer to those actions whose output is intended to be an improvement to an existing process.

Possible choices:

Taguchi Loss

Ishikawa

Kaizen

Kaizen Blitz

Muda

Scrum

Poka-yoke

None of the choices.

ANSWER:

Kaizen Events refer to those actions whose output is intended to be an improvement to an existing process. In fact they are commonly referred to as a tool for gathering operators, managers, and owners of a process in one place; mapping the existing process using tools such as deployment flowchart; improving the existing process; and soliciting buy-in from all the relevant parties.

Question 19

The main goal of TPS is to eliminate several major kinds of waste, including (choose all that apply):

Possible choices:

Over-production

Motion

Waiting

Conveyance

Processing Itself

Inventory

Correction

Standardization

None of the choices.

ANSWER:

Toyota Production System (TPS) can be thought of as Toyota's system of Lean manufacturing. The main goal of TPS is to eliminate 7 major kinds of waste, which are Over-production, Motion (of operator or machine), Waiting (of operator or machine), Conveyance, Processing Itself, Inventory (raw material), 7. Correction (rework & scrap).

Question 20

Which of the following is a Japanese term that refers to any activity that is wasteful and doesn't add value or is unproductive?

Possible choices:

Taguchi Loss

Ishikawa

Kaizen

Kaizen Blitz

Muda

Scrum

Poka-yoke

None of the choices.

ANSWER:

Muda is a Japanese term generally referring to any activity that is wasteful and doesn't add value or is unproductive. It is in fact a key concept in the Toyota Production System (TPS) and is one of the three identified types of waste.

Question 21

Which of the following is an iterative incremental framework for managing complex work?

Possible choices:

Taguchi Loss

Ishikawa

Kaizen

Kaizen Blitz

Muda

Scrum

Poka-yoke

None of the choices.

ANSWER:

Scrum is an iterative incremental framework for managing complex work. This is a term commonly used with agile software development, even though it can be used as a general project/program management approach as well.

Question 22

With _____ you are trying to avoid inadvertent errors.

Possible choices:

Taguchi Loss

Ishikawa

Kaizen

Kaizen Blitz

Muda

Scrum

Poka-yoke

None of the choices.

ANSWER:

Poka-yoke means "fail-safing" or "mistake-proofing". With Poka-yoke you are trying to avoid inadvertent errors. You can think of it as a method of preventing errors by putting limits on how an operation can be performed so to force the correct completion of an operation. Such a concept was originated by Shigeo Shingo as part of the TPS.

Question 23

The ADRI Cycle:

Possible choices:

is widely used in the private sector.

is widely used in the public sector.

is widely used in the non-profit sector.

is replaced by Six Sigma.

None of the choices.

ANSWER:

The ADRI Cycle is an essential tool in any improvement system and is widely used in the private sector. The cyclical nature of continuous improvement, more commonly referred to as the Quality Cycle, is well established and dominates most quality systems.

Question 24

The ADRI cycle has what specific stages (choose all that apply):

Possible choices:

Approach

Deployment

Results

Improvement

Recycle

Waste treatment

None of the choices.

ANSWER:

The ADRI cycle concentrates on improvement initiatives as well as the links between its four specific stages:

1. Approach – looks at how goals are to be achieved.

2. Deployment – looks at how the approach is to be put into action.

3. Results – looks at how well the deployment is being achieved.

4. Improvement – identifies and implements strategies and mechanism for improvements based on the previous ADRI stages.

Question 25

Which of the following often leads to a major revision in processes or the development of a new process?

Possible choices:

ADRI Cycle

SPC

quality circle

Breakthrough projects

Small-step projects

Control chart

Shewhart chart

None of the choices.

ANSWER:

There are two major types of continuous improvement project. Breakthrough projects often lead to a major revision in processes or the development of a new process resulting in a marked change in process measures. They are usually conducted by small cross-functional groups. Small-step projects, on the other hand, are ongoing activities that lead to a gradual change in process measures.

Question 26

Which of the following hinges on the observation that any manufacturing process is subject to seemingly random variations?

Possible choices:

ADRI Cycle

SPC

quality circle

Breakthrough projects

Small-step projects

Control chart

Shewhart chart

None of the choices.

ANSWER:

SPC is a method for achieving quality control in manufacturing processes. It hinges on the observation that any manufacturing process is subject to seemingly random variations, which are said to have common causes, and non-random variations, which are said to have special causes.

Question 27

Which of the following refers to a volunteer group of workers who regularly meet together to discuss workplace improvement initiatives?

Possible choices:

Pareto charts

SPC

quality circle

Breakthrough projects

Small-step projects

Control chart

Scatter diagrams

Shewhart chart

ANSWER:

A quality circle refers to a volunteer group of workers who regularly meet together to discuss workplace improvement initiatives. Typical topics include improving safety, improving product design, and improvement in manufacturing process. It has the advantage of continuity, and can quite effectively motivate and enrich the work life of your fellow employees.

Question 28

With _____, the main quality improvement process consists of the intentional varying of the production process to achieve a smaller range of control limits.

Possible choices:

Pareto charts

SPC

quality circle

Breakthrough projects

Small-step projects

Control chart

Scatter diagrams

Shewhart chart

ANSWER:

With SPC, the main quality improvement process consists of the intentional varying of the production process to achieve a smaller range of control limits.

Question 29

Which of the following is a plot of measurements of a product on two special scales, usually located above and below each other and running horizontally?

Possible choices:

Pareto charts

SPC

quality circle

Breakthrough projects

Small-step projects

Control chart

Scatter diagrams

Shewhart chart

ANSWER:

A control chart is a plot of measurements of a product on two special scales, usually located above and below each other and running horizontally. The purpose of any control chart is to help determine if variations in measurements of a product are caused by small, normal variations that cannot be acted upon, or by some larger special cause that can be acted upon or fixed.

Question 30

Which of the following is also known as XbarR chart?

Possible choices:

Pareto charts

SPC

quality circle

Breakthrough projects

Small-step projects

Control chart

Scatter diagrams

Shewhart chart

ANSWER:

The type of chart to be used is based on the nature of the data. The most commonly used process control charts include XbarR chart (i.e. the Shewhart chart), P Chart; NP Chart; C Chart; and U Chart. Each of these charts has a specific area of application.

Question 31

Control chart cannot prevent unnecessary process adjustments.

Possible choices:

True

False

ANSWER:

False. Control chart is preferable for describing precisely what is meant by statistical control. It is quite effective in defect prevention and can prevent unnecessary process adjustments.

Question 32

Which of the following can be helpful for graphically depicting the influence that one variable has on another?

Possible choices:

Pareto charts

Zero Defects

Quality circle

Failure testing

Scorecarding

Control chart

Scatter diagrams

Shewhart chart

ANSWER:

Pareto charts (which are a form of bar charts) are useful for identifying those factors that have the greatest cumulative effect. Scatter diagrams are helpful for graphically depicting the influence that one variable has on another.

Question 33

The P chart:

Possible choices:

is highly sensitive to changes in the proportion of defective items in the measurement process.

is highly insensitive to changes in the proportion of defective items in the measurement process.

ANSWER:

The P chart is similar to the C chart. It is highly sensitive to changes in the proportion of defective items in the measurement process. The "P" in fact stands for the proportion of successes of a binomial distribution.

Question 34

Pre-Control is a technique for monitoring whether a process remains in statistical control on the basis of what attribute data (choose all that apply):

Possible choices:

red

yellow

green

blue

black

None of the choices.

ANSWER:

According to the ASQ, Pre-Control (a.k.a. stoplight control) is a technique for monitoring whether a process remains in statistical control on the basis of three-level attribute data, which is coded as red, yellow, or green, all basing on a set of specification limits. Simply put it is a quality monitoring scheme similar to a control chart.

Question 35

Which of the following refers to the notional quality standard developed by Phil Crosby which has been primarily adopted within industry supply chains?

Possible choices:

Pareto charts

Zero Defects

Quality circle

Failure testing

Scorecarding

Control chart

Scatter diagrams

Shewhart chart

ANSWER:

"Zero Defects" refers to the notional quality standard developed by Phil Crosby which has been primarily adopted within industry supply chains wherever large volumes of components are being purchased for further production use.

Question 36

With _____ you test the operation of a product until it fails.

Possible choices:

Pareto charts

Zero Defects

Quality circle

Failure testing

Scorecarding

Control chart

Scatter diagrams

Shewhart chart

ANSWER:

Failure testing is often conducted on consumer products. With failure testing, you test the operation of a product until it fails, often under extreme stresses of all sorts. The goal is to expose the unanticipated weaknesses in a product.

Question 37

Which of the following is an approach which uses multiple related measures to ascertain whether or not success has been achieved?

Possible choices:

Pareto charts

Zero Defects

Quality circle

Failure testing

Scorecarding

Control chart

Scatter diagrams

Shewhart chart

ANSWER:

Scorecarding is an approach which uses multiple related measures to ascertain whether or not success has been achieved. Typically an organization will define a number of key strategic objectives. These measures are plotted on a single piece of paper to represent a scorecard of achievement.

Question 38

ISO 9000:

Possible choices:

is a standard for ensuring a product or service is of quality.

is not a standard for ensuring a product or service is of quality.

ANSWER:

ISO 9000 specifies requirements for a Quality Management System overseeing the production of a product or service. It is not a standard for ensuring a product or service is of quality. It is a standard attesting to the process of production and how it will be managed and reviewed.

Question 39

ISO _____ exists to ensure that the manufacture of a product has the lowest possible environmental ramifications.

Possible choices:

9000

9001

14000

15000

16000

None of the choices.

ANSWER:

ISO 14000 exists to ensure that the manufacture of a product has the lowest possible environmental ramifications. Similar to ISO 9000, it is pertaining to the product production process only.

Question 40

The Malcolm Baldrige National Quality Award:

Possible choices:

recognizes top-quality U.S. companies.

recognizes top-quality U.K. companies.

recognizes top-quality worldwide companies.

ANSWER:

The Malcolm Baldrige National Quality Award is a competition that identifies and recognizes top-quality U.S. companies. It addresses a broadly based range of quality criteria, including commercial success and corporate leadership.

Question 41

Which of the following outlines the general requirements a laboratory must meet to be recognized as competent to carry out tests and calibrations?

Possible choices:

ISO/IEC Guide 25

QS-9000

VDA 6.1

EAQF

AVQS

ISO-16000

AS-9000

None of the choices.

ANSWER:

ISO/IEC Guide 25 outlines the general requirements a laboratory must meet to be recognized as competent to carry out tests and calibrations. Calibration generally refers to the process of determining the relation between the output of a measuring instrument and the value of the input quantity or attribute, following a measurement standard.

Question 42

Which of the following specifically affects major and minor manufacturing customers in the US automobile industry?

Possible choices:

ISO/IEC Guide 25

QS-9000

VDA 6.1

EAQF

AVQS

ISO-16000

AS-9000

None of the choices.

ANSWER:

Developed by General Motors, Chrysler and Ford, QS-9000 specifically affects major and minor manufacturing customers in the automobile industry in the US. The standard is divided into 3 sections.

Question 43

ISO (TR) 16949 attempts to harmonize (choose all that apply):

Possible choices:

ISO/IEC Guide 25

QS-9000

VDA 6.1

EAQF

AVQS

ISO-16000

AS-9000

None of the choices.

ANSWER:

ISO (TR) 16949 is an effort by the Big Three U.S. automakers in cooperation with European automakers to harmonize four source documents: QS-9000 (United States), VDA 6.1 (Germany), EAQF (France) and AVQS (Italy).

Question 44

Which of the following aims to assure the organization receives full value for every dollar invested?

Possible choices:

VE

IE

RE

SE

TE

ME

None of the choices.

ANSWER:

As a branch of industrial engineering, Value Engineering (VE) is used to assure the organization receives full value for every dollar invested. VE techniques are used to improve productivity in nearly every aspect of operation in the organization, including practices, processes and procedures.

Question 45

Methods Engineering is a sub category of:

Possible choices:

VE

IE

RE

SE

TE

ME

None of the choices.

ANSWER:

Methods Engineering is a sub category of Industrial engineering. It is primarily concerned with human integration among different industrial production processes. In fact, the terms operation analysis, work design and simplification, and methods engineering and corporate re-engineering are frequently used interchangeably.

Question 46

Which of the following refers to the analysis of a specific job by a qualified worker in an effort to find the most efficient method in terms of time and effort?

Possible choices:

Quality Study

Time Study

Resource Study

Field Study

Process capability

Standard Time Data

Work Measurement Study

None of the choices.

ANSWER:

Time Study and Methods Engineering are kind of related. Time Study refers to the analysis of a specific job by a qualified worker in an effort to find the most efficient method in terms of time and effort. It aims at measuring the time necessary for a job or task to be completed using the best method.

Question 47

Which of the following describes the systematic application of industrial engineering techniques to establish the work content and time it should take to complete a task or series of tasks?

Possible choices:

Quality Study

Time Study

Resource Study

Field Study

Process capability

Standard Time Data

Work Measurement Study

None of the choices.

ANSWER:

Work Measurement Study describes the systematic application of industrial engineering techniques to establish the work content and time it should take to complete a task or series of tasks. It is a productivity improvement tool.

Question 48

Which of the following is all about the collection of time values?

Possible choices:

Quality Study

Time Study

Resource Study

Field Study

Process capability

Standard Time Data

Work Measurement Study

None of the choices.

ANSWER:

Standard Time Data is all about the collection of time values. It uses work elements from time studies or other work measurement sources making it unnecessary to restudy work elements that have been timed adequately in the past. All the element times would be extracted from studies and applied to jobs with the same element(s).

Question 49

In the context of RMM, the drivers for the systematic progression of levels include variables such as (choose all that apply):

Possible choices:

Process Management

Risk Appetite Management

Uncovering Risks

Business Resiliency

Sustainability

Confidentiality

None of the choices.

ANSWER:

The RMM maturity ladder is organized progressively from "ad hoc" to "leadership" which depicts corresponding levels of risk management competency. The drivers for the systematic progression of levels are termed as "Attributes" and include variables such as Process Management, Risk Appetite Management, Uncovering Risks, and Business Resiliency and Sustainability.

Question 50

Which of the following deals with the repeatability and consistency of a manufacturing process relative to the customer requirements, primarily in terms of specification limits of a product parameter?

Possible choices:

Quality Study

Time Study

Resource Study

Field Study

Process capability

Standard Time Data

Work Measurement Study

None of the choices.

ANSWER:

Process capability deals with the repeatability and consistency of a manufacturing process relative to the customer requirements, primarily in terms of specification limits of a product parameter. This measure aims to objectively measure the degree to which your process is or is not meeting the requirements.

Question 51

Which of the following allows you to place the distribution of your process in relation to the product specification limits?

Possible choices:

Probability

Field resource indices

Process capability

Capability indices

Standard Time Data

Work Measurement Study

None of the choices.

ANSWER:

Capability indices allow you to place the distribution of your process in relation to the product specification limits. You want to use capability indices to determine whether the process, given its natural variation, is capable of meeting established specifications.

Question 52

Cp and Cpk are the measurements of:

Possible choices:

Probability

Field resource indices

Process capability

Capability indices

Standard Time Data

Work Measurement Study

None of the choices.

ANSWER:

Cp and Cpk are the measurements of process capabilities. They are often used in studies such as process capability and can be used to monitor a process, just like how X-Bar and Range charts are used.

Question 53

Probability theory has its primary concern on the analysis of:

Possible choices:

random phenomena

time data

short term trend

long term trend

None of the choices.

ANSWER:

Probability theory is a branch of mathematics, with primary concern on the analysis of random phenomena. The central objects of probability theory include random variables, stochastic processes, and events.

Question 54

In probability theory, what is the counterpart to a deterministic process?

Possible choices:

random phenomena

stochastic process

time trend process

short term trending

long term trending

None of the choices.

ANSWER:

In probability theory, a stochastic process is sometimes being referred to as random process. It is the counterpart to a deterministic process - instead of handling only one possible "reality" of how the process might evolve, in a random process there is some indeterminacy in its future evolution described by probability distributions.

Question 55

Which of the following deals with events that occur in countable sample spaces?

Possible choices:

Discrete probability theory

Independence probability theory

Dependence probability theory

Random probability theory

None of the choices.

ANSWER:

Discrete probability theory deals with events that occur in countable sample spaces. Independence probability theory says that two events are independent intuitively, which means that the occurrence of one event would make it neither more nor less probable that the other occurs.

Question 56

Discrete distributions that are considered as fundamental include which of the following (choose all that apply):

Possible choices:

discrete uniform

bernoulli

binomial

negative binomial

poisson

geometric

None of the choices.

ANSWER:

Certain random variables can occur very often in probability theory simply due to the fact that they well describe many natural or physical processes. Discrete distributions that are considered as fundamental include discrete uniform, Bernoulli, binomial, negative binomial, Poisson and geometric distributions. On the other hand, continuous distributions that are deemed important include continuous uniform, normal, exponential, gamma and beta distributions.

Question 57

Which of the following is a manufacturing strategy in which parts are produced or delivered only as needed?

Possible choices:

Pareto charts

Kanban

quality circle

DPU

DPMO

Control chart

Scatter diagrams

Shewhart chart

None of the choices.

ANSWER:

Kanban is a manufacturing strategy in which parts are produced or delivered only as needed. Toyota Motor has been credited with developing the Kanban system, which takes its name from the Japanese word for "sign" or "placard".

Question 58

Which of the following refers to inspections for defects which count the number of defects that can occur on a specified number of units of product?

Possible choices:

Pareto charts

Kanban

quality circle

DPU

DPMO

Control chart

Scatter diagrams

Shewhart chart

None of the choices.

ANSWER:

Defects Per Unit (DPU) refers to inspections for defects which count the number of defects that can occur on a specified number of units of product.

Question 59

Which of the following is a method for measuring process performance and serving as a basis for calculating process sigma values?

Possible choices:

Pareto charts

Kanban

quality circle

DPU

DPMO

Control chart

Scatter diagrams

Shewhart chart

None of the choices.

ANSWER:

Defects per Million Opportunities (DPMO) is a method for measuring process performance. It can serve as a basis for calculating process sigma values as well.

Question 60

PDPC is a technique quite popular for developing:

Possible choices:

contingency plans

test plans

sampling plans

quality plans

new product development plans

None of the choices.

ANSWER:

Process Decision Program Chart (PDPC) is a technique quite popular for developing contingency plans. Its emphasis is to identify the consequential impact of failure on activity plans, and create appropriate contingency plans to limit risks.

Question 61

Relations Diagrams are drawn for showing all the different relationships between (choose all that apply):

Possible choices:

factors

areas

processes

people

descriptive statistics

probability

None of the choices.

ANSWER:

Interrelationship Digraphs are also known as Relations Diagrams. They are drawn for showing all the different relationships between factors, areas, or processes. They make it easy to pick out the factors in a situation which are the ones that are driving the other symptoms and factors.

Question 62

What are the most common measures of variability (choose all that apply):

Possible choices:

Heterogeneity

Variance

Standard Deviation

Normal Distribution

Regression Analysis

None of the choices.

ANSWER:

The two most common measures of variability, namely the Variance and the Standard Deviation, owe their popularity to the importance of the Normal Distribution, which is completely determined by their mean and their variance. The variance describes the heterogeneity of a distribution and is calculated from a formula that involves every score in the distribution.

Question 63

A histogram that is perfectly symmetrical around its middle:

Possible choices:

has no skewness.

has positive skewness.

has negative skewness.

is part of the Queuing Theory

None of the choices.

ANSWER:

Skewness refers to the asymmetry of a histogram. If the histogram is perfectly symmetrical around its middle, the it has no skewness. If, on the other hand, the histogram has a hump toward the left and the right-hand tail stretches out longer than the left-hand tail, then the distribution is positively skewed.

Question 64

Statistical inference combines the methods of (choose all that apply):

Possible choices:

descriptive statistics

probability

factors

areas

processes

people

None of the choices.

ANSWER:

Statistical inference combines the methods of descriptive statistics with the theory of probability to learn what samples of data tell about the characteristics of populations from which they were drawn. You will want your drawn sample to be representative of the population if it is to reflect on the population's characteristics.

Question 65

Interval Estimation is a form of:

Possible choices:

statistical inference

normal distribution

descriptive statistics

probability

factors

areas

queuing theory

None of the choices.

ANSWER:

Interval Estimation is a form of statistical inference. It produces an interval of values by a process that has a known probability of including the true but unknown parameter value on the interval. The interval is known as a confidence interval.

Question 66

Markov analysis provides a means of analyzing state transition:

Possible choices:

when strong dependencies are exhibited.

when strong dependencies are absent.

ANSWER:

Markov analysis provides a means of analyzing state transition when strong dependencies are exhibited.

Question 67

Which of the following enables you to quantify the relationship between two or more variables by fitting a line or plane through all the points?

Possible choices:

Heterogeneity

Variance

Standard Deviation

Normal Distribution

Regression Analysis

None of the choices.

ANSWER:

Queuing Theory deals with problems which involve queuing and waiting. Regression analysis enables you to quantify the relationship between two or more variables by fitting a line or plane through all the points such that they are evenly distributed about the line or plane.

Question 68

Which of the following is the average time between failures of a system?

Possible choices:

MTBF

MTRF

MTSF

MTCF

MTTF

MTBCF

MTBUR

None of the choices.

ANSWER:

Mean time between failures (MTBF) is the average time between failures of a system. It is typically part of a model that assumes the failed system is immediately repaired (in other words, there is no elapsed time).

Question 69

Which of the following is a measure of the average time between failures with the modeling assumption that the failed system is not going to get repaired?

Possible choices:

MTBF

MTRF

MTSF

MTCF

MTTF

MTBCF

MTBUR

None of the choices.

ANSWER:

Mean time to failure (MTTF) is a measure of the average time between failures with the modeling assumption that the failed system is not going to get repaired.

Question 70

You need to have the client informed of the quality audit through:

Possible choices:

audit contract

engagement letter

audit plan

initial meeting

preliminary survey

None of the choices.

ANSWER:

You need to have the client informed of the audit through an announcement or engagement letter. Such a letter communicates the scope and objectives of the audit, the auditors assigned to the project and other relevant information.

Question 71

Which of the following is the tool the auditor uses to gather relevant information about the target unit in order to obtain a general overview of operations?

Possible choices:

audit contract

engagement letter

audit plan

initial meeting

preliminary survey

None of the choices.

ANSWER:

Preliminary Survey is the tool the auditor uses to gather relevant information about the target unit in order to obtain a general overview of operations.

Question 72

Which of the following establishes the contract between the auditing department and the organization?

Possible choices:

audit charter

engagement letter

audit plan

previsit meeting

preliminary survey

None of the choices.

ANSWER:

Developing a charter for the audit department is important because it establishes the contract between the auditing department and the organization. Yet, care should be taken to ensure that the charter serves its purpose of documenting the understanding between the two.

Question 73

The ability of any audit function to achieve audit objectives depends largely on:

Possible choices:

scope of work.

specifications.

independence.

budget.

None of the choices.

ANSWER:

The ability of any audit function to achieve audit objectives depends largely on its independence.

Question 74

The auditor should express an opinion on a subject:

Possible choices:

only when it is based on reasonable estimate or honest conviction

only when it is based on adequate knowledge and honest conviction

only when it is based on proper quantitative assessment.

ANSWER:

The auditor should express an opinion on a subject only when it is based on adequate knowledge and honest conviction. Opinions when given should be solidly grounded in objective evidence.

Question 75

An auditor should not accept gifts or entertainment of a nature or degree that might possibly prejudice the audit or affect the relationship between the auditee and the audit team:

Possible choices:

no matter what

unless the value is less than USD$20

unless the value is less than USD$30

unless the value is less than USD$50

unless the value is less than USD$100

None of the choices.

ANSWER:

An auditor should not accept gifts or entertainment of a nature or degree that might possibly prejudice the audit or affect the relationship between the auditee and the audit team. Dollar value does not matter.

Question 76

Every quality system should include (choose all that apply):

Possible choices:

management policies

objectives

documentation

performance of tasks

corrective action

None of the choices.

ANSWER:

Every quality system should include: management policies; objectives; an organization; documentation; performance of tasks according to policies; monitoring of the system (feedback) and corrective action as indicated by the feedback.

Question 77

During Control Review you primarily want to determine (choose all that apply):

Possible choices:

the areas of lowest risk

the areas of highest risk

the areas of average risk

ANSWER:

During Control Review the auditor reviews the target unit's existing control structure. To save time, the auditor uses a variety of tools and techniques to gather and analyze information about the operation. One primary objective here is to determine the areas of highest risk and design tests to be performed in the fieldwork section.

Question 78

A risk-based quality audit program:

Possible choices:

is often based on an effective scoring system

is often based on budget.

is often based on scope.

is often based on an scale of the organization.

None of the choices.

ANSWER:

A risk-based quality audit program is often based on an effective scoring system which is supported by top management.

Question 79

Which of the following will list the actions taken by the client to resolve the original report findings?

Possible choices:

Corrective Suggestion

Action Plan

Unbiased Opinion

Follow-up Report

None of the choices.

ANSWER:

A Follow-up Report will list the actions taken by the client to resolve the original report findings.

Question 80

Which of the following is primarily used in the US food industry for identifying potential food safety hazards?

Possible choices:

MSDS

HACCP

ISO 12000

Orange Book

6 Sigma

None of the choices.

ANSWER:

HACCP is primarily used in the US food industry for identifying potential food safety hazards, so that key actions can be taken to reduce or eliminate the risk of the hazards being realized. The system is being implemented at all stages of food production and preparation processes.

Question 81

With HACCP, what indicates a condition that constitutes a major dysfunction likely to result in a potential compromise to food safety?

Possible choices:

CLE

CLA

CLR

CCF

CCP

None of the choices.

ANSWER:

With HACCP, a Critical Listing Element (CLE) is an item marked during an audit, indicating a condition that constitutes a major dysfunction likely to result in a potential compromise to food safety.

Question 82

With HACCP, what refer to those steps at which control can be applied and a food safety hazard can be prevented, eliminated or reduced effectively?

Possible choices:

CLE

CLA

CLR

CCF

CCP

None of the choices.

ANSWER:

With HACCP, Critical Control Points (CCP) refer to those steps at which control can be applied and a food safety hazard can be prevented, eliminated or reduced effectively. Complete and accurate identification of CCPs is critical to controlling food safety hazards.

END OF BOOK

Made in the USA
San Bernardino, CA
13 March 2017